The Big Boo

Stupendous, mind-boggl to send your senses reeling, your eyes whirling and your brain cells haywire!

THE BIG BOOK OF OPTICAL ILLUSIONS

A CAROUSEL BOOK 0 552 54155 9

First publication in Great Britain

PRINTING HISTORY
Carousel edition published 1979

*Carousel Books are published by
Transworld Publishers Ltd.,
Century House, 61-63 Uxbridge Road,
Ealing, London W5 5SA.*

Made and printed in Great Britain by the Guernsey Press Co., Ltd., Guernsey, Channel Islands.

THE BIG BOOK OF OPTICAL ILLUSIONS

Gyles Brandreth

Optical Illusions and Amazing Mazes
by Albert Murphy
Cartoons by Rowan Barnes Murphy

CAROUSEL BOOKS
A DIVISION OF TRANSWORLD PUBLISHERS LTD.

other books by GYLES BRANDRETH

DOMINO GAMES AND PUZZLES
NUMBER GAMES AND PUZZLES
GAMES AND PUZZLES WITH COINS AND MATCHES
PENCIL AND PAPER GAMES AND PUZZLES
HOTCHPOTCH
THE ROYAL QUIZ BOOK
BRAIN TEASERS AND MIND-BENDERS
EDWARD LEAR'S BOOK OF MAZES
BIG BOOK OF SECRETS
PUZZLE PARTY FUN BOOK
THE DAFT DICTIONARY
JOKES, JOKES, JOKES: A JOKE FOR EVERY DAY OF THE YEAR
THE GREAT BIG FUNNY BOOK
PROJECT: THE HUMAN BODY
PROJECT: NUMBER FUN
BIG BOOK OF PRACTICAL JOKES

All published by CAROUSEL BOOKS

STOP!

Life is full of surprises—and so is this book. In it you're going to find all sorts of things that aren't quite what they seem.

To begin with, take a close look at this shape:

You will agree that no one could possibly describe that shape as a perfect circle? Good. Now look at the picture of the bicycle on the next page. How would you describe the shape of the bicycle's front wheel? You would describe it as a circle, would you? Of course you would, because you **know** that a bicycle wheel has a circular shape.

The artist drew exactly the same line to make the shape above—that obviously isn't a circle—as he did to make the bicycle wheel—that obviously is a circle! But while you are looking at the same shape on both this page and the next, you understand that the bicycle wheel has to be circular even when it doesn't seem to be.

What I'm talking about is a very complicated phenomenon that is called **perception.** Perception is turning what we see into what we understand. Our perception is our view of the world. It's our perception that tells us the first shape looks a bit like an elongated egg and the second looks like the circular wheel of a bicycle.

It's our perception that tells us that the word SUNSHINE is written here—

when actually it isn't.

You were able to read the word SUNSHINE even though it wasn't written there—and it really wasn't—because the black shadows made the word appear. The shadows enabled you to **perceive** the word, in the same way that these few shadows enable you to perceive the clear outline of a bird:

Usually, we see what we expect to see, but sometimes our perception lets us down and we perceive something to be so that isn't actually so! That should happen to you quite a few times as you look through this book, because optical illusions very often manage to fool your perception and make you begin to wonder if seeing is believing after all.

FIRST ILLUSION

What's this?

An elegant vase or two old men?

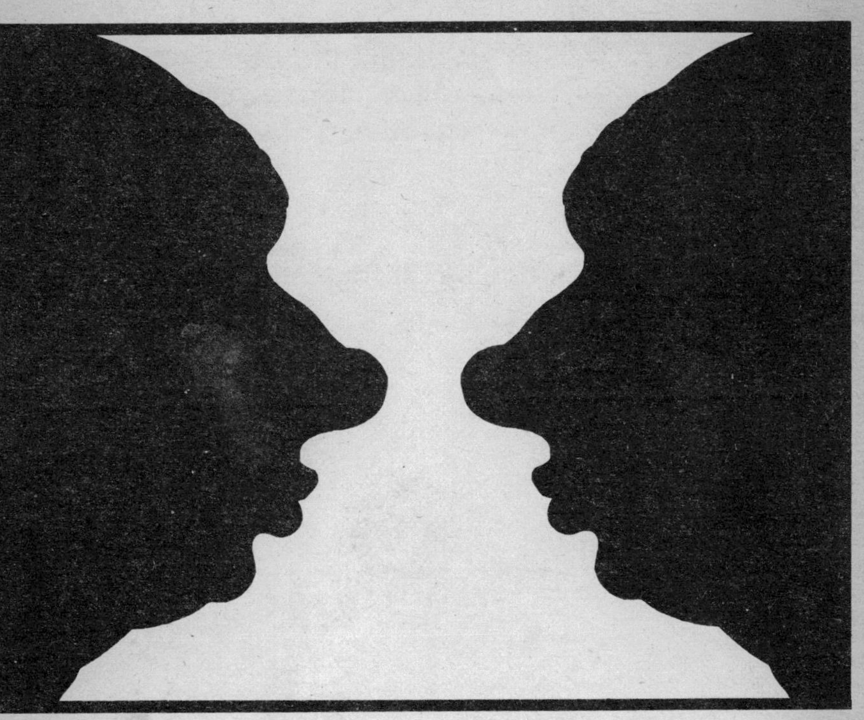

It's both, of course. Concentrate on the white area and you'll see the vase. Concentrate on the black and the two men will appear.

GREAT GAZE

Gaze at the pattern on the facing page for at least a minute.

Then look at a perfectly blank wall and you'll find that you start seeing strange little moving specks on the wall.

It's very odd, but don't let it frighten you!

FIVE FIELDS

Here are five fields.

Which is the largest and which is the smallest?

All five fields are exactly the same size. The different shapes make them appear to be different sizes.

TWO BRICKS

This white brick is a little bigger

than this white brick

—isn't it?

No. Both bricks are the same size. If they look unequal in size it's because of the black lengths on either side of them.

SURPRISE YOUR EYES

Which is bigger:
A or B?

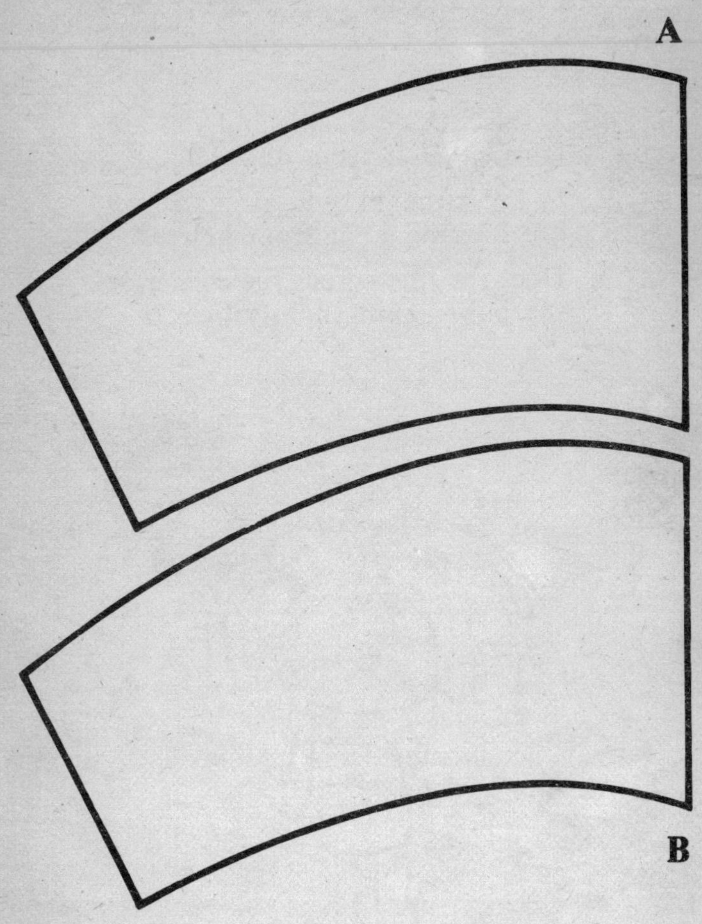

Wrong again! They're both the same size.

CURIOUS CUBE

Look carefully at the picture opposite then try to answer these three questions:

1. Is the cube on a table and you are looking at it from above?
2. Is the cube in mid-air and you are looking at it from below?
3. Does the line across the corner of the cube seem slightly bent?

You could be looking at the cube from above **or** *below! Sometimes you will feel you're looking up at the cube from below and sometimes you will feel you are looking down on the cube from above.*

The line does seem to be slightly bent, but it isn't. It's perfectly straight.

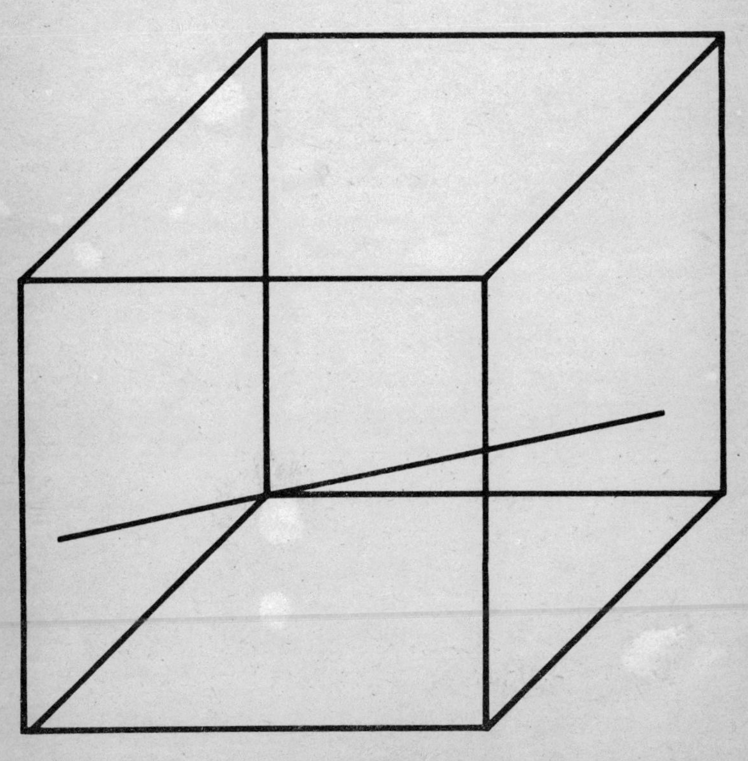

CENTRE POINT

Glance at the facing page and say what you can see right in the middle of it.

If you said you saw the letter B that's because you first perceived the horizontal line of letters A, B, C. If you said you saw the number 13 that's because you first perceived the vertical line of numbers, 12, 13, 14.

12

A 13 C

14

ROUND AND ROUND

Look at either of these two circles.

Concentrate on one and revolve the book. Turn it round and round as quickly as you can.

When you stop, for a moment the pattern will suddenly seem to go round in the opposite direction.

IMPOSSIBLE!

Whichever way you look at it this is an 'impossible' object.

It is possible to draw it on paper, but you could never build it out of wood. And if it looks normal to you, look again — starting at the base of the object and then letting your eye move up it.

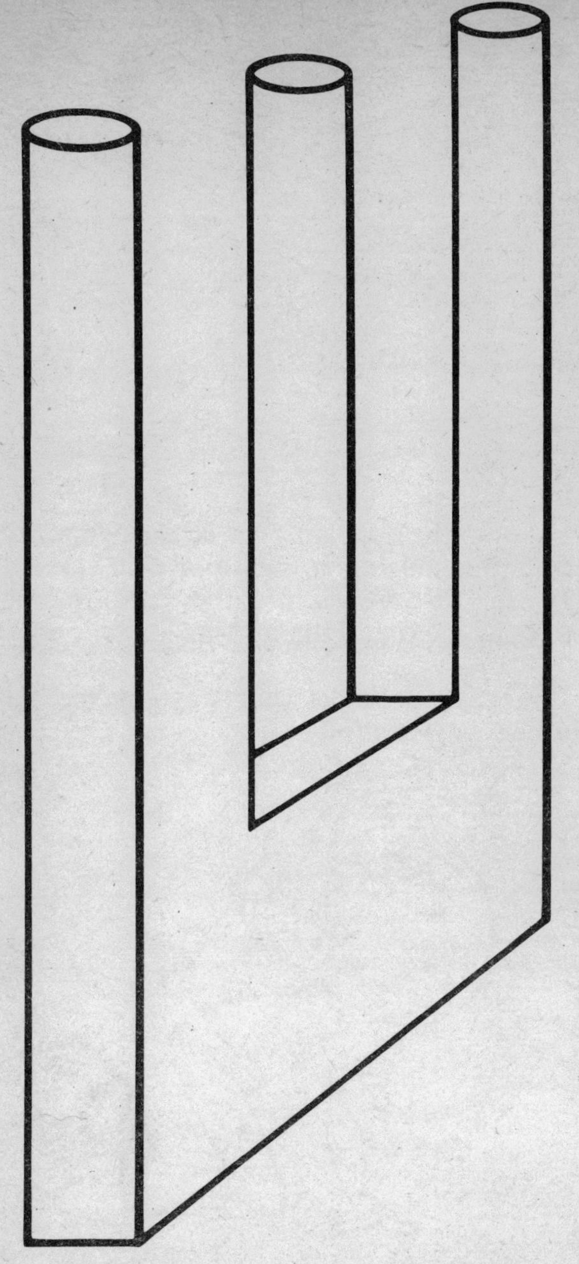

X MARKS THE SPOT

Look at the spot marked X and you will find that the dots in the square on the left appear in **rows** while the dots in the square on the right appear in **columns.**

It always happens that way—never the other way around!

RIGHT ANGLES?

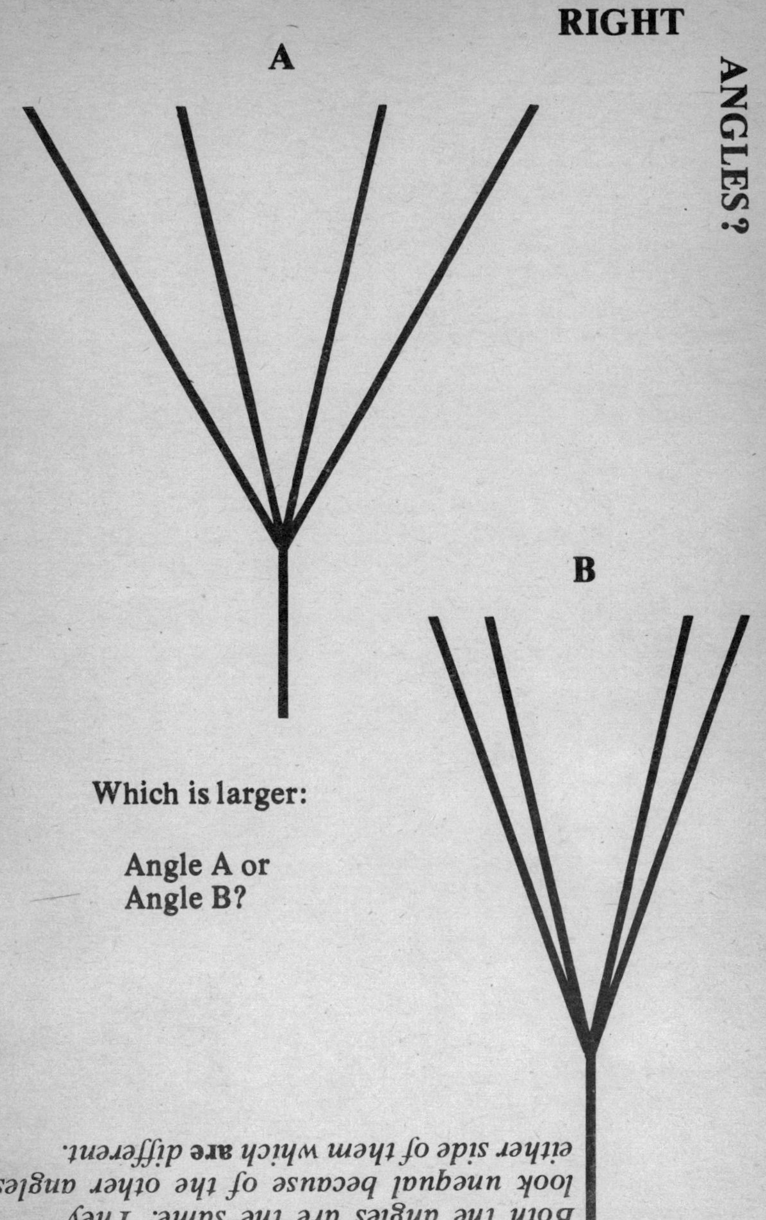

Which is larger:

**Angle A or
Angle B?**

Both the angles are the same. They look unequal because of the other angles either side of them which **are** *different.*

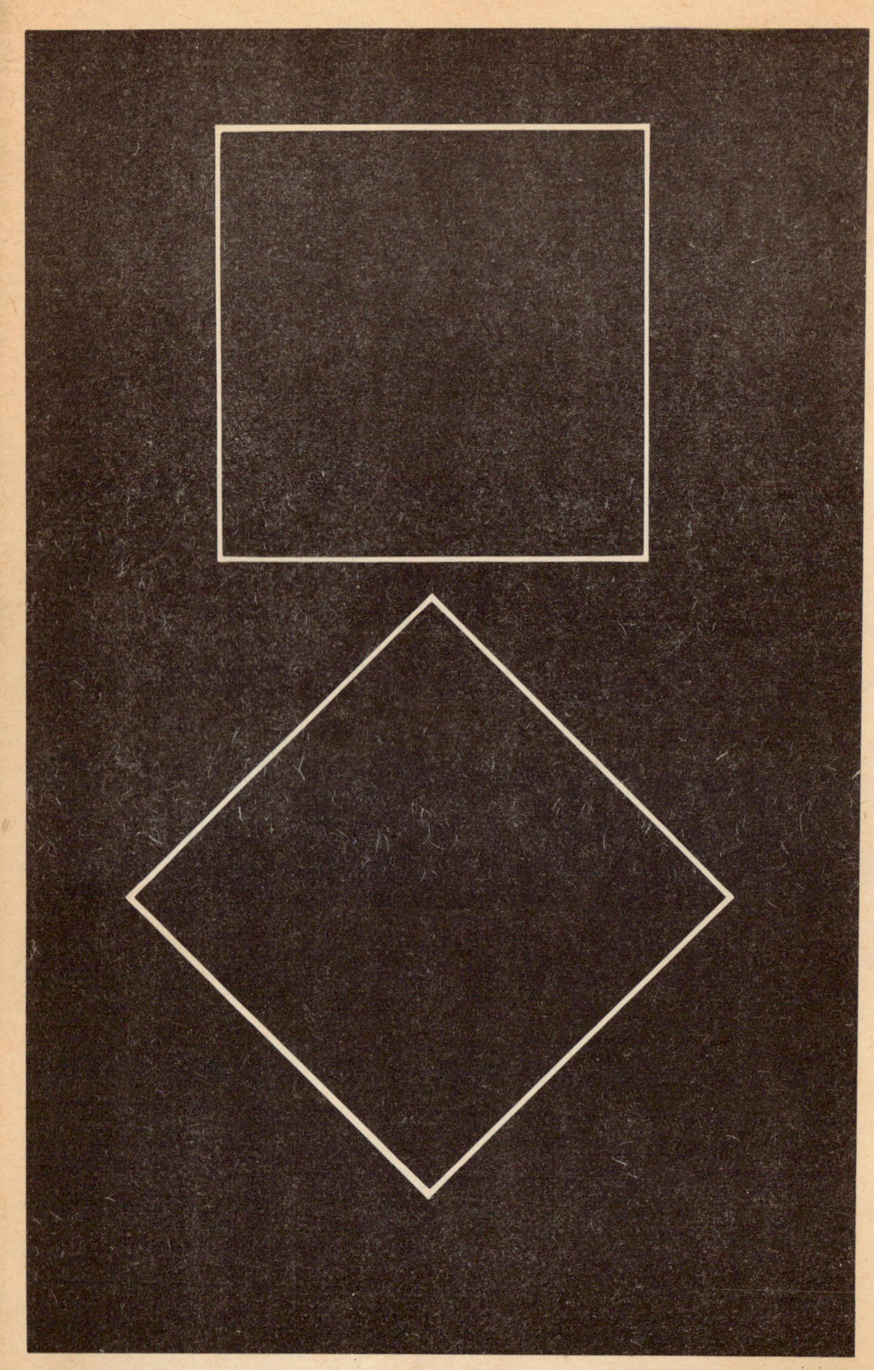

DIAMONDS AND SQUARES

Which is bigger:

the diamond or
the square?

They are both the same size, but a square will seem larger when tilted on one side and viewed like a diamond.

EYE DAZZLER

Look at the facing page for long enough and your mind will really begin to boggle.

What can you see? Rows of triangles? Rows of pigeon-holes? Rows of open boxes seen from above? Or a mixture of different patterns that keep changing as you look at them?

HOW FAR?

Is B nearer to A or nearer to C?

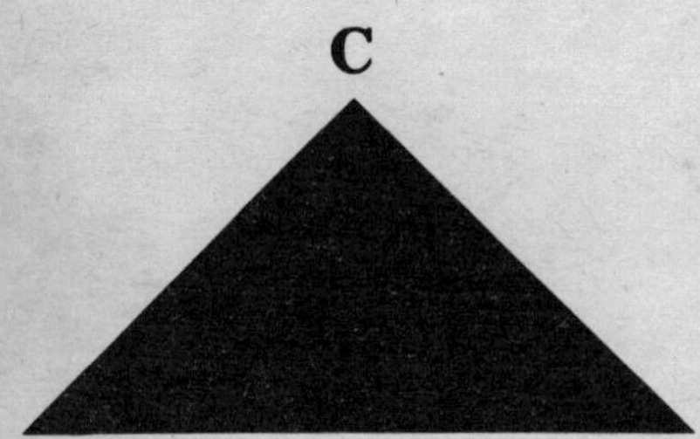

B looks a lot nearer A, doesn't it? In fact, B is exactly midway between A and C so the distance between A and B and B and C is identical.

WHAT'S WHAT?

What's this a picture of?

There's more to the picture than two lines, two black spots and a curve. The picture shows a cleaning lady on her knees scrubbing the floor with her bucket of water beside her. Now you **know** *what's in the picture you'll have no problem seeing it, will you?*

SQUARE WORLD

One of these two areas is very slightly larger than the other.

Which is it?

The white square seems a little larger than the black square, but in fact they're both exactly the same size.

TILE AND ERROR

Look at this wall of black and white tiles.

Why do you think they weren't put on straight?

They were! The rows of tiles are perfectly straight. Admittedly they don't look it, but put a ruler to them and you'll see they are.

WATCH THEM BEND!

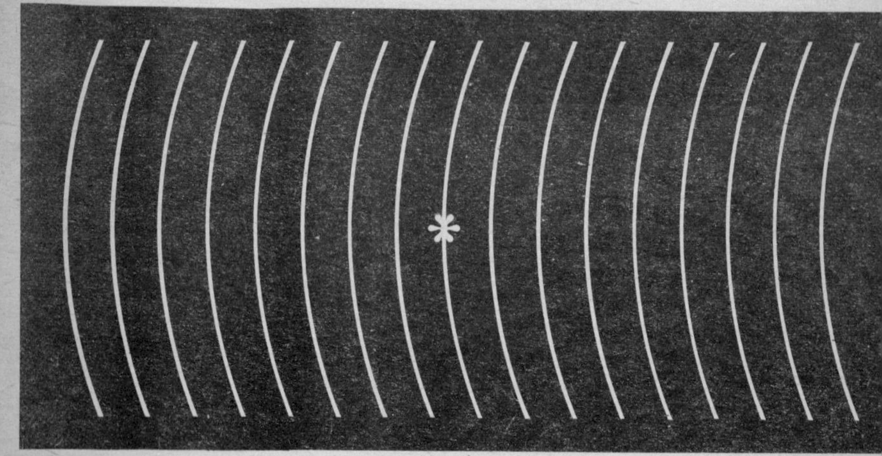

Look at the star on this page steadily while you count to 100 very slowly.

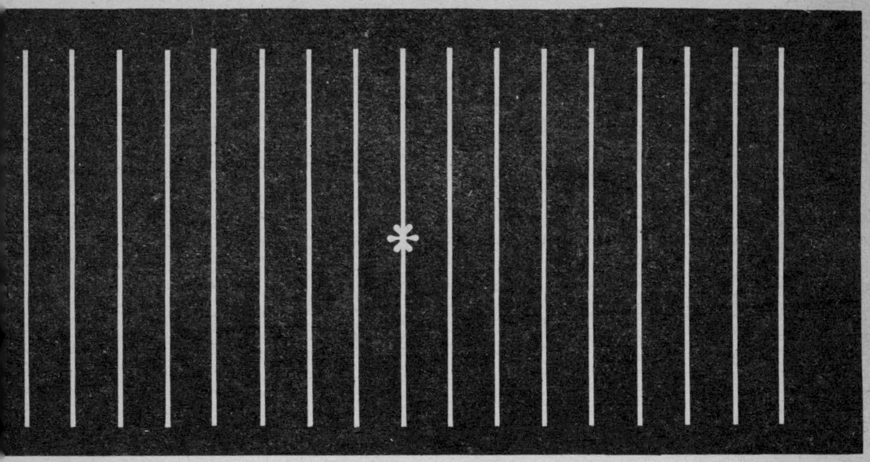

Now look at the star on this page and watch the lines curve in the opposite direction!

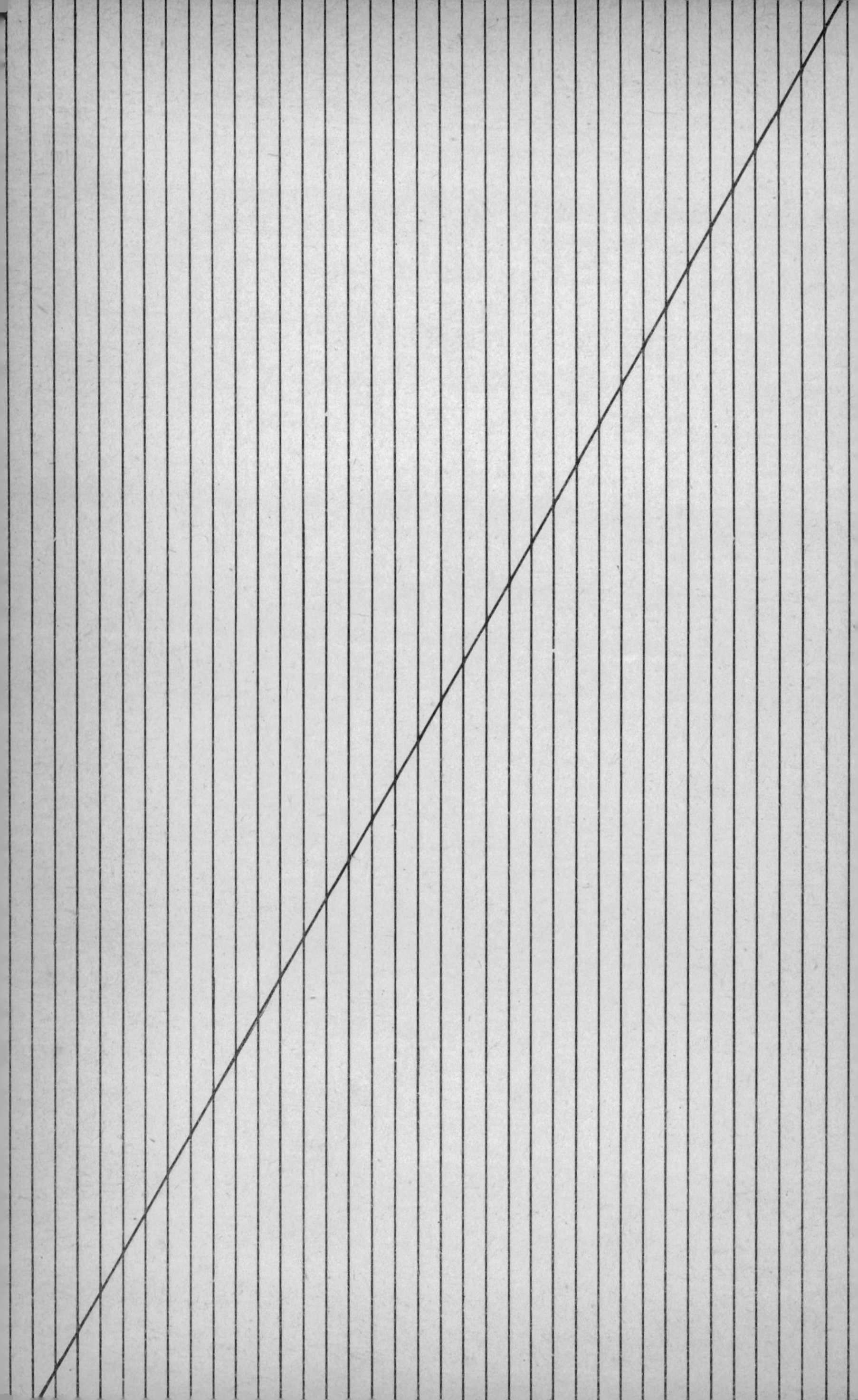

INS AND OUTS

Look carefully at the diagonal line on the facing pace.

Is it straight? Or does it twist in and out of the horizontal lines and seem a bit jagged?

The diagonal line is quite straight. The vertical lines behind it make it seem distorted.

UP OR DOWN?

You will have to turn the book sideways to see this strange figure properly. And when you do look at it, are you seeing it from above or below?

This is one of those odd figures that you feel you are seeing from above at one moment and from below at the next. Whichever way you look at it, it's still confusing!

A QUESTION OF LINES

Which of the three straight lines is the longest: the top one, the middle one or the bottom one?

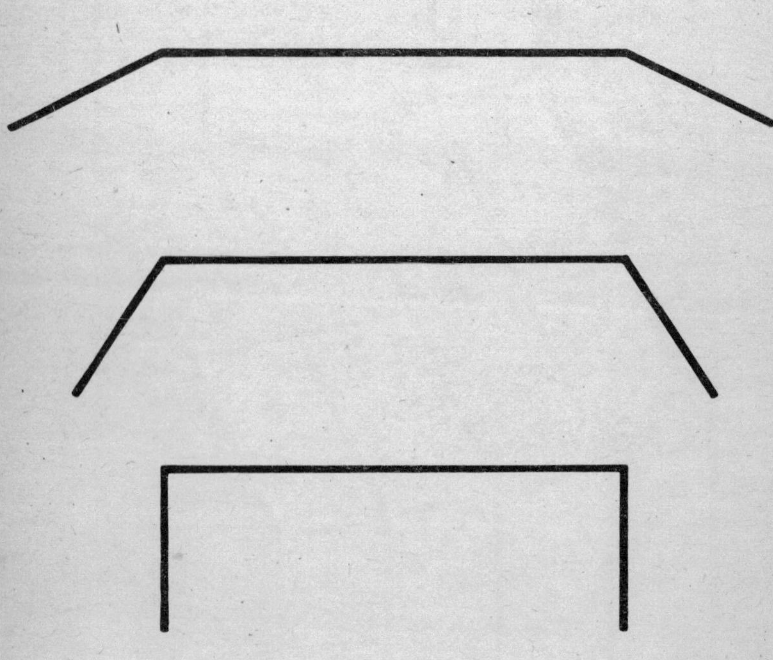

All three are the same length. It is the angles that make the straight parts of the lines look different lengths.

A QUESTION OF ANGLES

Which is the longer line:

the one from A to C

or

the one from B to D?

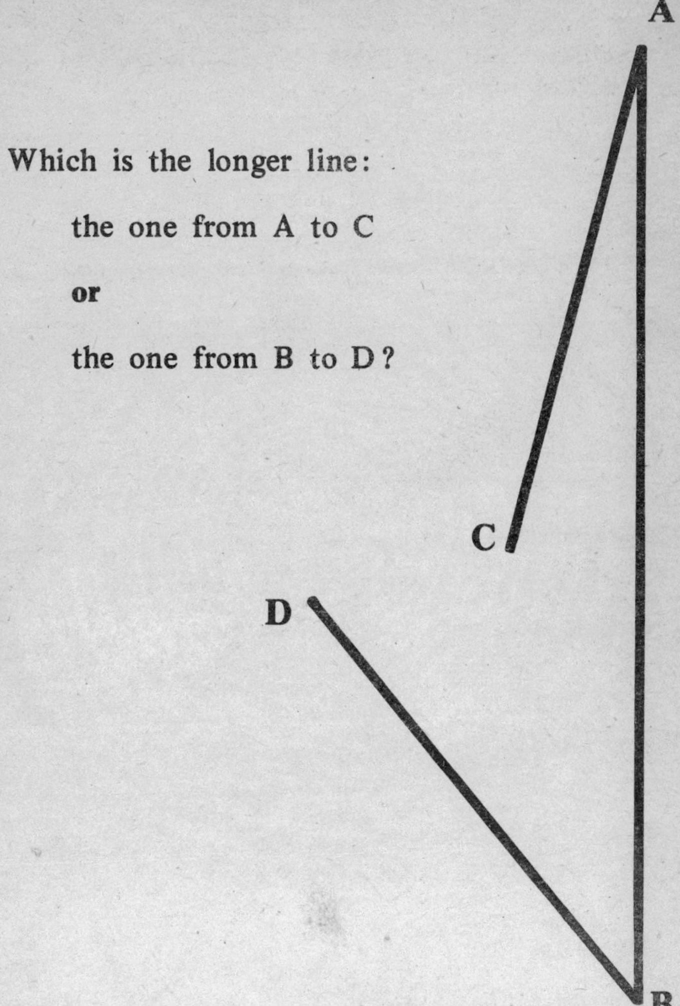

Both lines are the same length. It is the angle they're at that makes them look different.

BULLSEYE

Revolve the pages and the spirals will seem to get bigger or smaller depending which way you are turning the page.

STRAIGHT AND NARROW

How many of the vertical lines on the facing page are bending this way and that? And how many of them are perfectly straight?

They are all quite straight. It is the pattern of wavy lines behind them that make them appear to bend.

HOW FAR THIS TIME?

A

B

Is the distance between A and B greater or smaller than the distance between C and D?

C

D

It looks greater, but in fact it's the same.

MASTER CARPENTER

Give a friend twelve pieces of wood and ask him to build this hollow crate for you. Tell him he can have £1,000 if he succeeds!

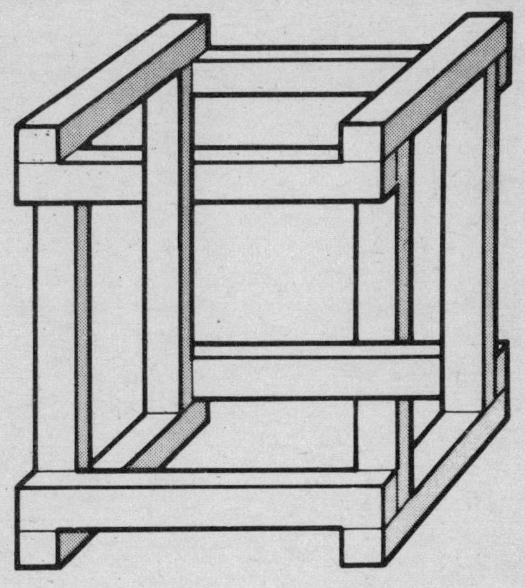

Don't worry, your money's safe. However skilled a carpenter your friend happens to be, he'll never build the crate. It's an impossible object.

SOME CIRCLES

Of the two centre circles, which one is the bigger?

They are both the same size. The top one only looks bigger because it is surrounded by smaller circles and the bottom one only looks smaller because it is surrounded by bigger circles.

COUNT DOWN

How many cubes can you count here?

The answer is 6 **or** *7. It will be 6 if you saw the patterned part as the* **top** *of each cube, but 7 if you saw the patterned part as the* **bottom** *of each cube.*

And if you found that mind-boggling, you can really get yourself confused by trying to find your way through the cube maze. Go in at one arrow and come out at the other.

POINTED

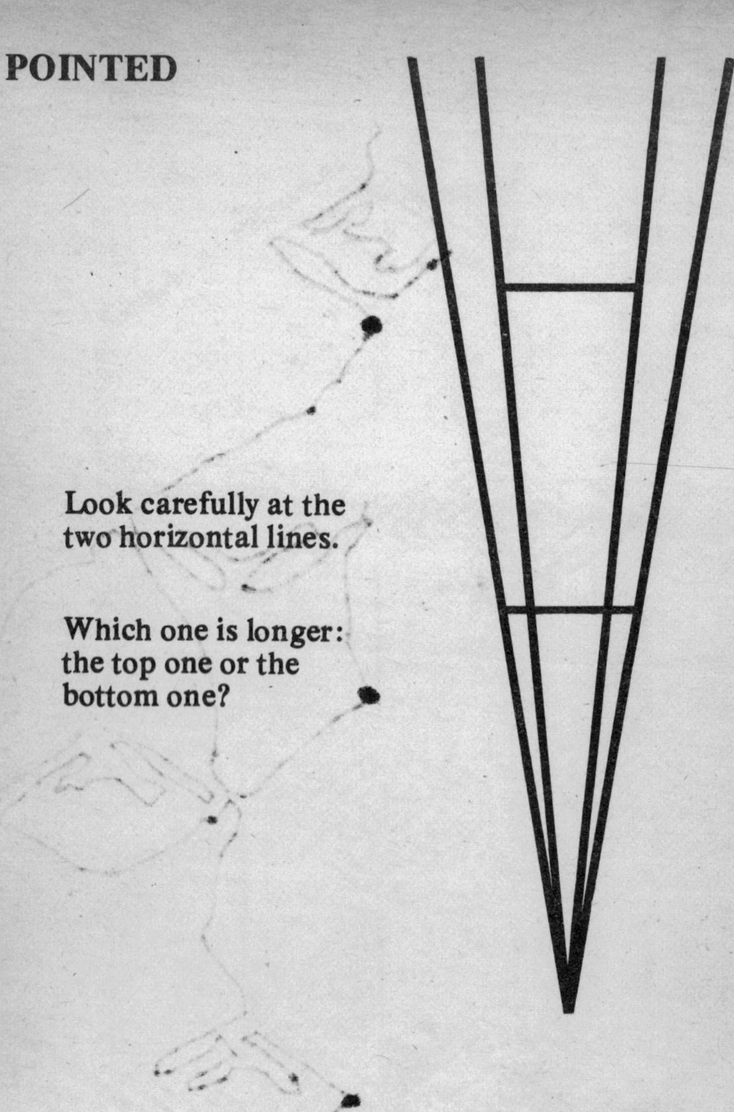

Look carefully at the two horizontal lines.

Which one is longer: the top one or the bottom one?

Both are exactly the same length. It's their positioning that makes the lower one look longer.

ARC ROYAL

Which of the three arcs is the biggest:

the top one,

the middle one,

or the bottom one?

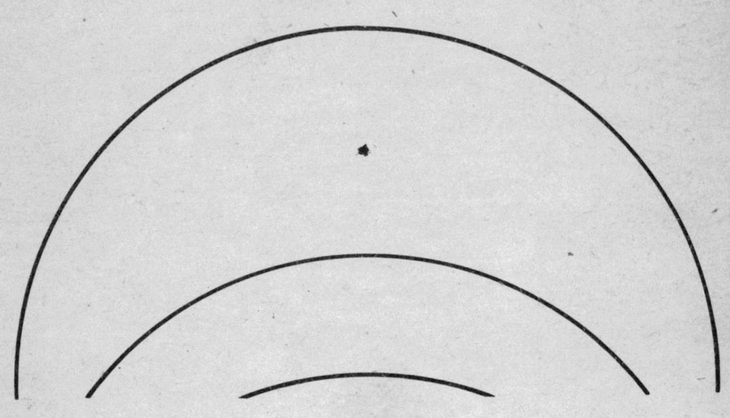

All three are arcs from exactly the same circle, but the more you see of each arc the greater the bend seems to be.

WHICH WAY?

Look carefully at the two vertical lines.

Do they bend inwards at the middle?

Do they bend outwards at the middle?

Or are they perfectly straight?

The lines look as if they bend inwards at the middle, but they don't. They are perfectly straight parallel lines.

FROM HERE TO THERE

Is the line from A to B longer or shorter than the line from C to D?

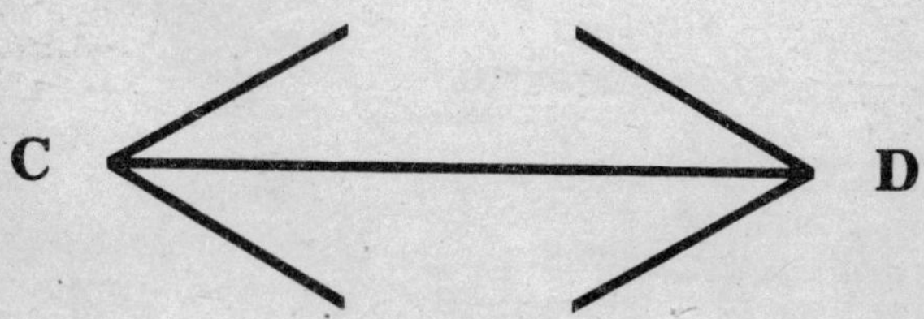

It looks longer, but both lines are actually the same length.

UP OR DOWN?

Where are you?

Are you up in the sky looking down on the roof of a house? Or are you in a room looking into a corner?

The answer is 'either'! The line in the middle will either appear nearer to you (the roof) or further away from you (the corner) — depending on how you see it!

REVOLVER

Look at the circle on the opposite page and keep looking at it. As you look at it, it will seem to revolve. (Don't look at it for too long, or you might begin to feel a bit dizzy!)

TAKE THE TUBE

Here's an unusual tube. Look carefully at it for at least a minute and then decide if you are looking down the tube from above it **or** up the tube from under it.

You can look at the tube either way. Sometimes you'll feel you're seeing through it from the top and sometimes from the bottom!

GREAT OR SMALL

Which of these two circles is the larger?

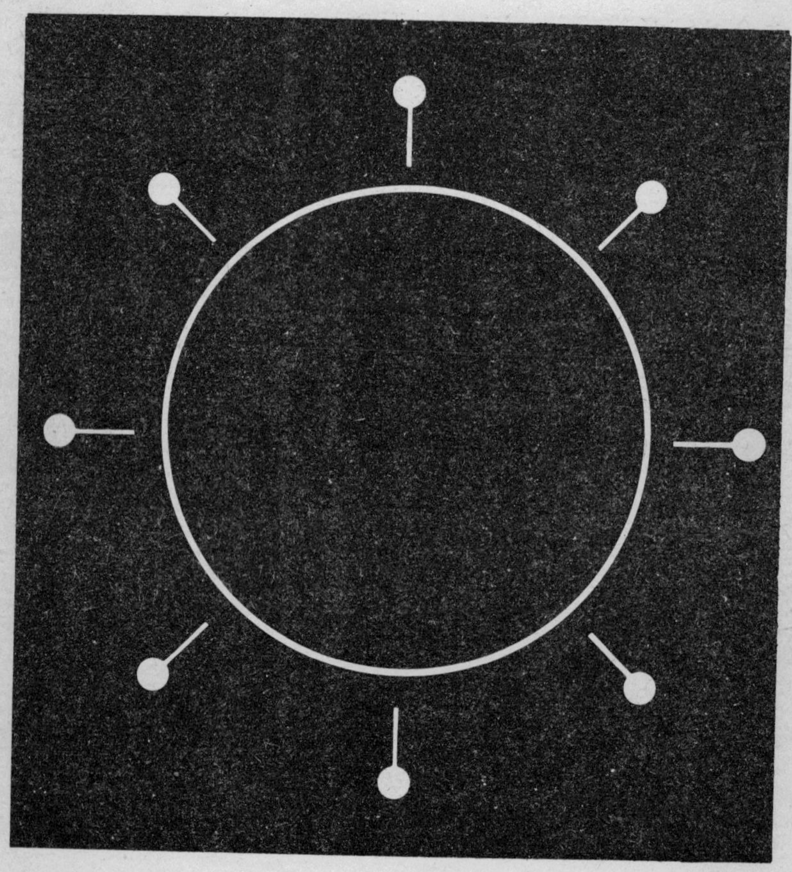

The one on this page?

Or the one on this page?

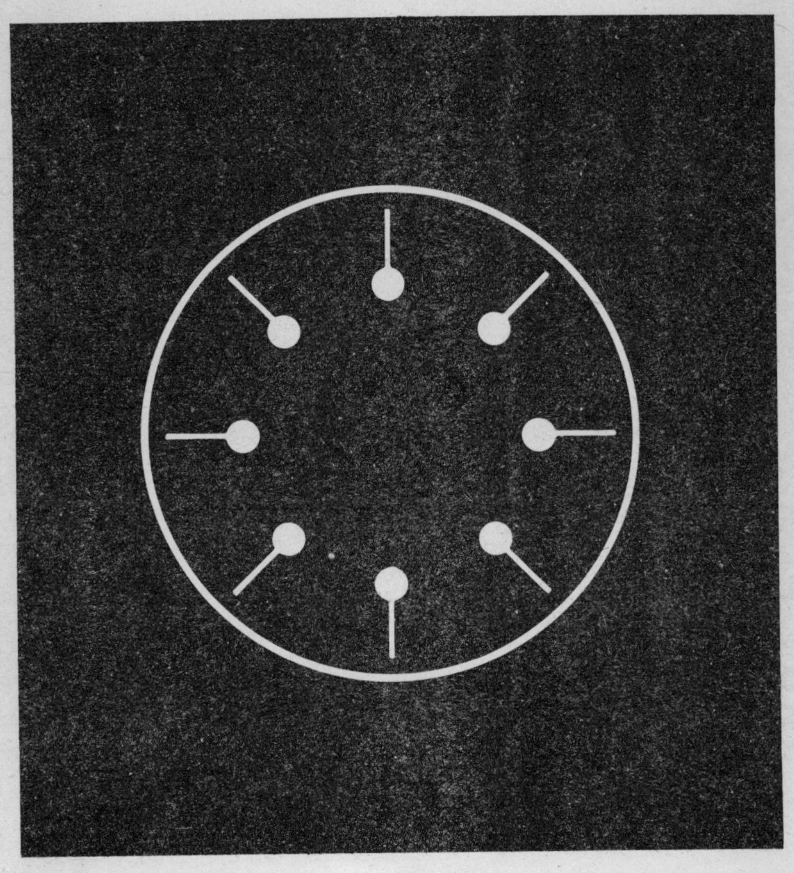

Well, you're wrong, the one on this page certainly looks smaller, but in fact both circles are identical in size.

TWO CIRCLES

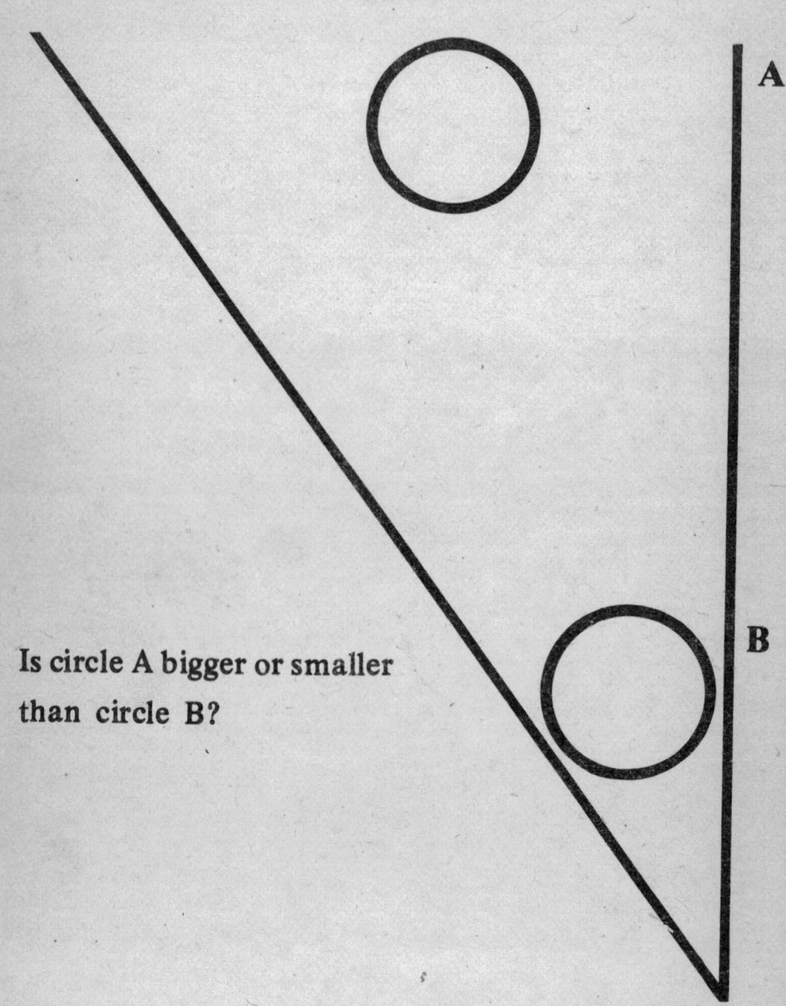

Is circle A bigger or smaller than circle B?

Both the circles are the same size. If they look different, it is because of their position inside the angle.

UPSTAIRS DOWNSTAIRS

Find the top step. And when you have found it, start looking for the bottom step.

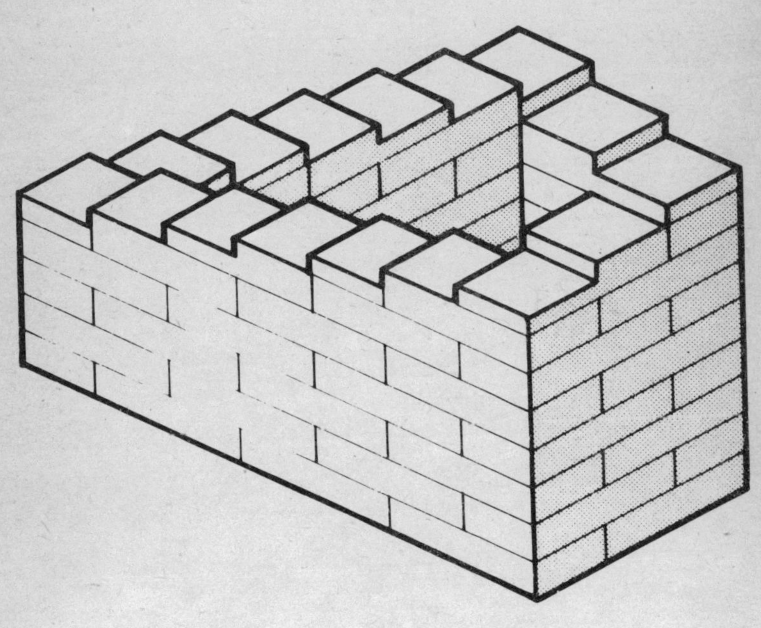

If you think you managed to find the top and bottom steps, you were wrong? They don't exist because the stairway is an impossibility!

CROSSROADS

Glance at the facing page and strange grey spots will appear at all the points where the lines cross. Look at any one crossing in particular and the grey spot that was there will suddenly disappear!

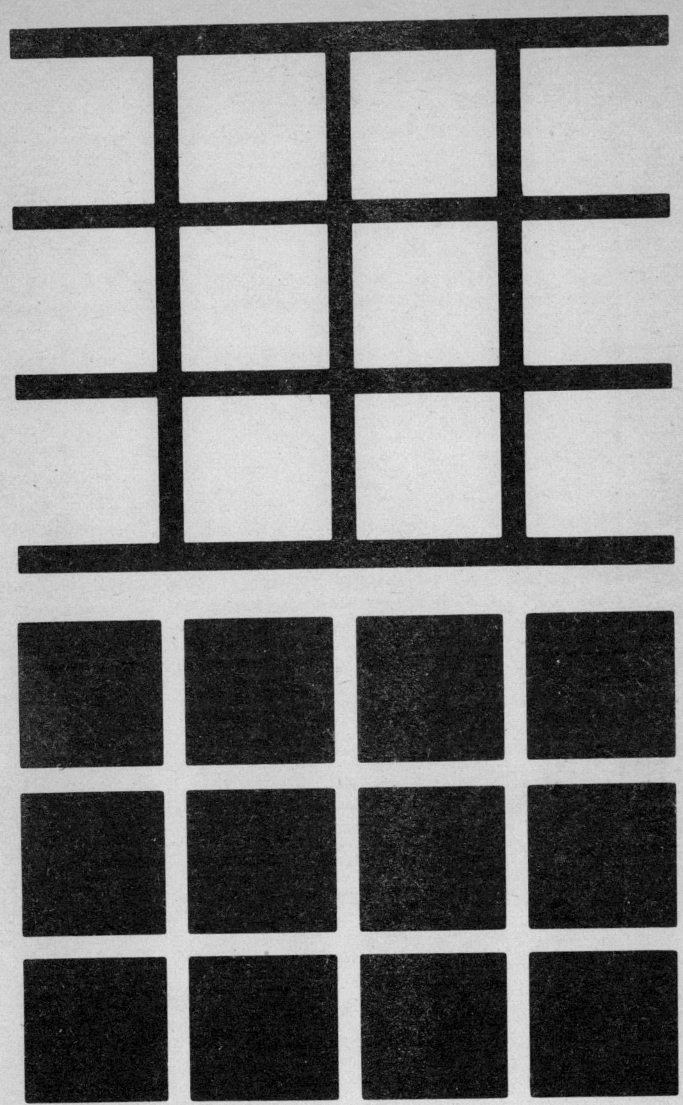

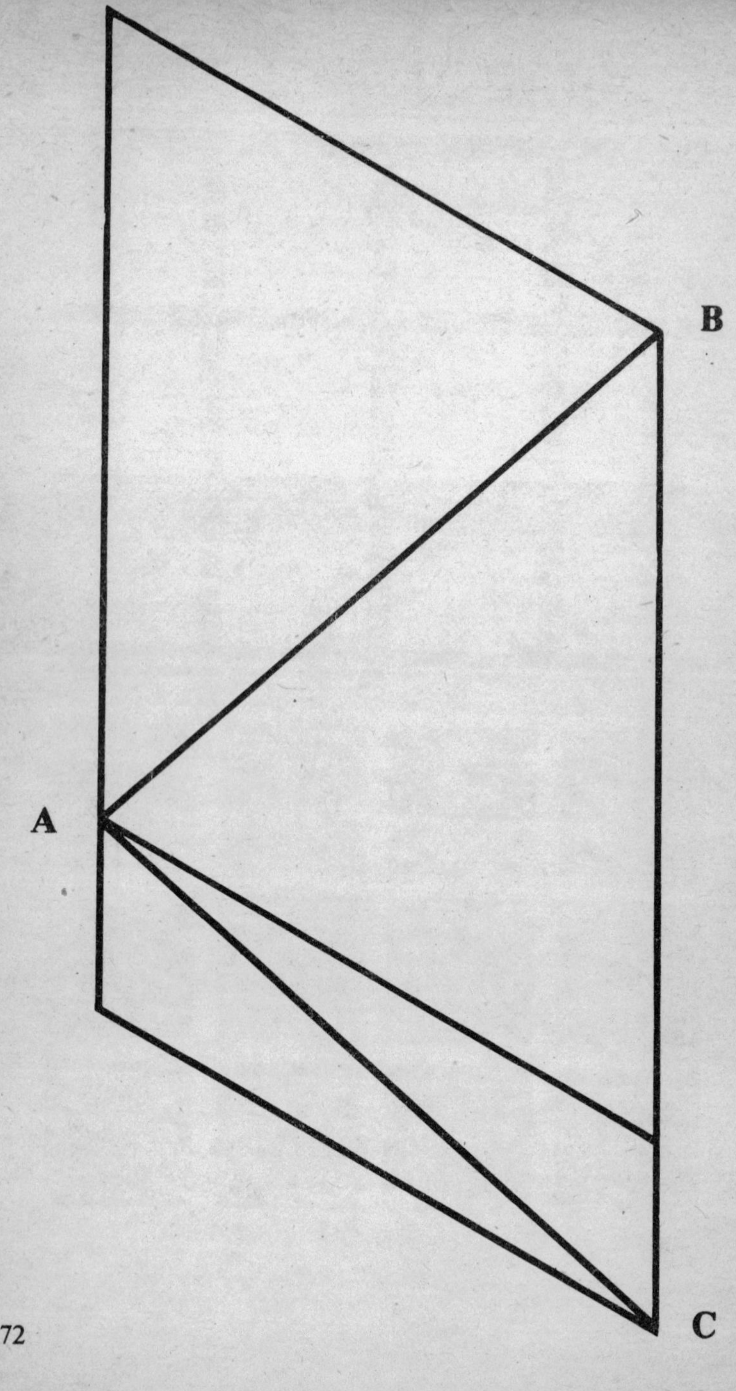
B
A
C

PARALLEL BARS

Look carefully at this parallelogram.

Which line is longer:
AB or AC?

AB looks a lot longer, but in fact both lines are the same length. Check with a ruler if you don't believe us.

GREY MATTER

Look at the three shades of grey in the circle and two rectangles and decide which of the three is darkest.

The bottom rectangle **looks** *darkest because it is set against a white background, but in fact all three grey areas are identical.*

ALL SQUARE

Of the three squares, which one is the smallest?

All three squares are identical. The ones with the vertical and horizontal lines in them just seem to occupy a larger area.

LONG AND LONGER

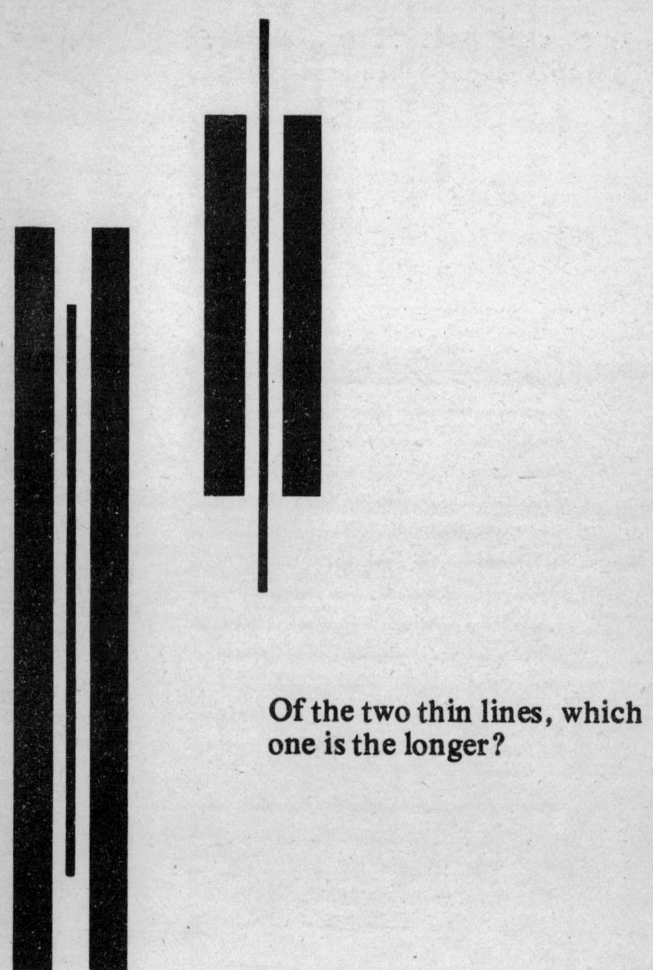

Of the two thin lines, which one is the longer?

The two thin lines are of equal lengths. They look different because of the different lengths of thick lines on either side of them.

CIRCULAR SAW

Why does each side of the square bend inwards slightly in the middle?

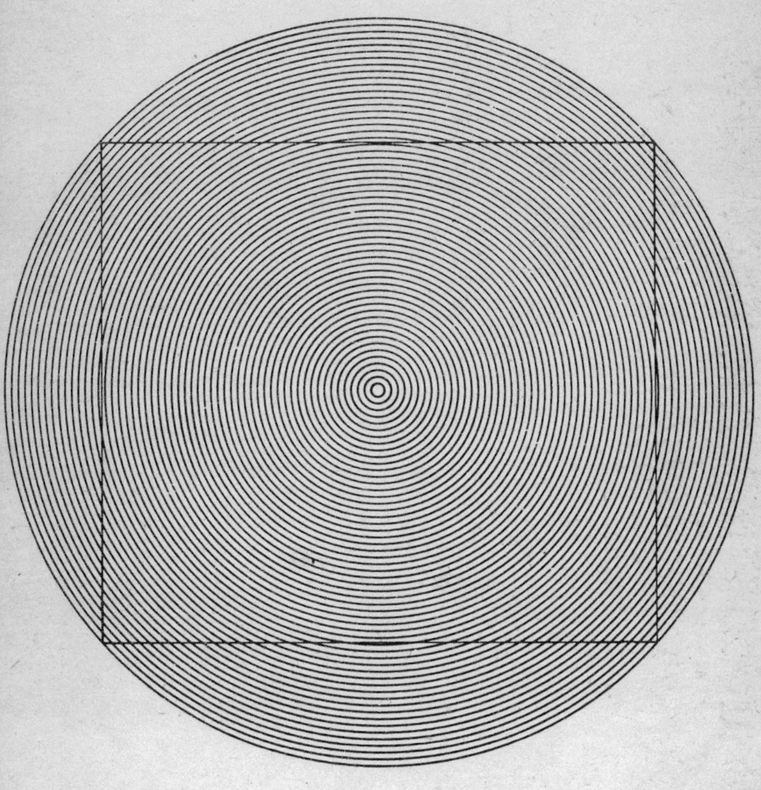

In fact, it's a perfect square. The sides don't bend at all. They just seem to because of the pattern of rings behind.

LITTLE AND LARGE

Which of the two circles is the larger?

A

A looks a little larger than B, but in fact both the circles are the same size. It's the position and size of the boxes that deceive you.

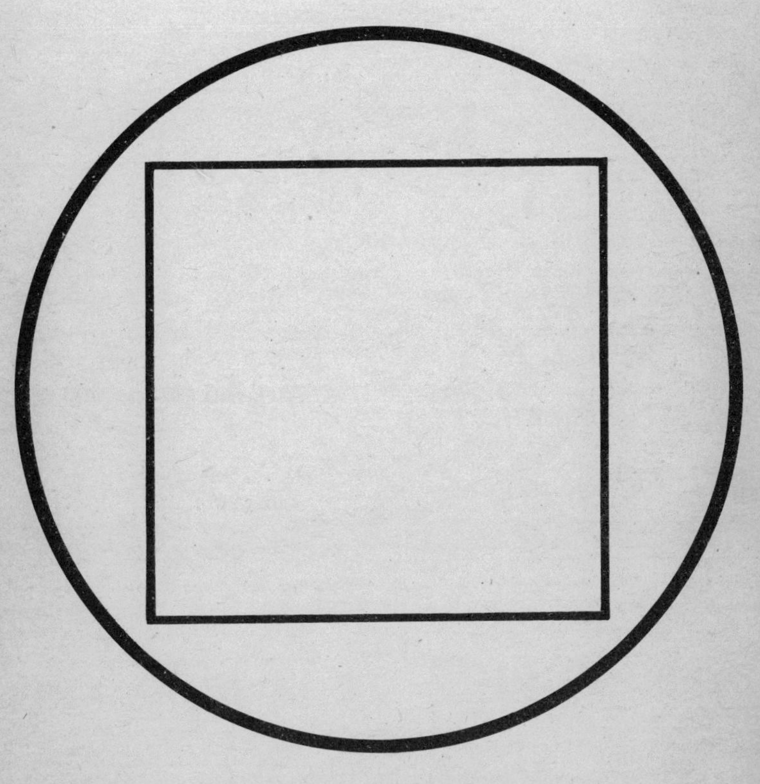

OUT OR IN?

Look carefully at the two vertical lines.

Do they bend outwards
in the middle?

Do they bend inwards
in the middle?

They don't bend at all! They are perfectly straight parallel lines.

WOODEN TRIANGLE

If you're any good at carpentry, have a go at making this simple wooden triangle.

Actually, don't! The wooden triangle is one of those 'impossible objects' that are quite easy to draw, but rather more difficult to make.

HONEYCOMB

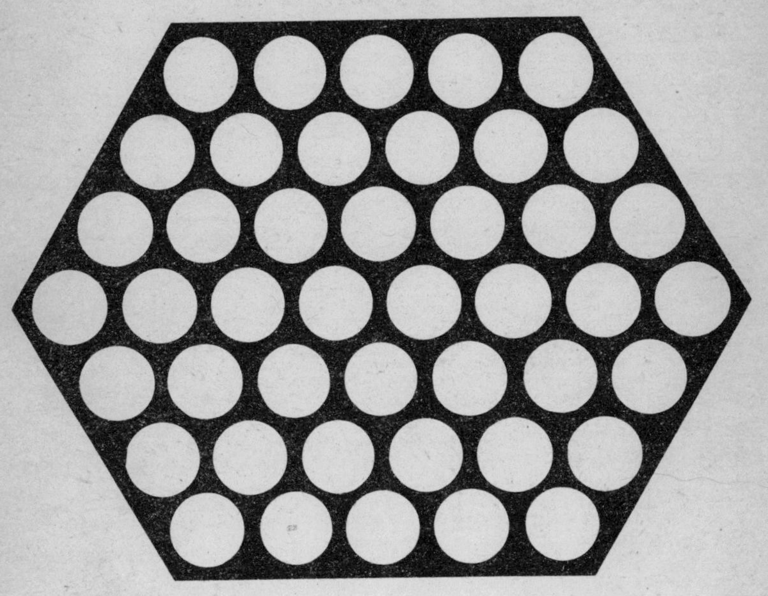

Look at this pattern long enough and you'll find the circles begin to look like hexagons.

LONG ROAD

Which of the two horizontal lines is the longer? It looks like the top one, but are you sure?

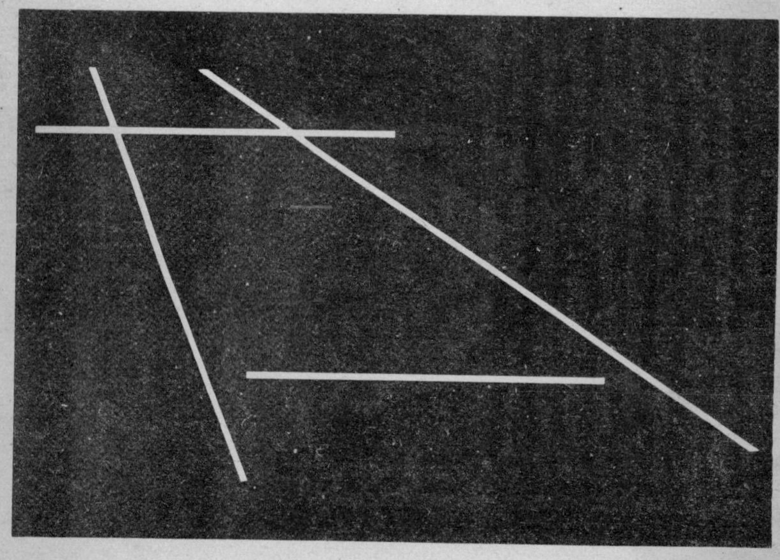

Both the horizontal lines are the same length. It's the converging lines that make the top line look longer.

ANIMAL MAGIC

What creature have we here?

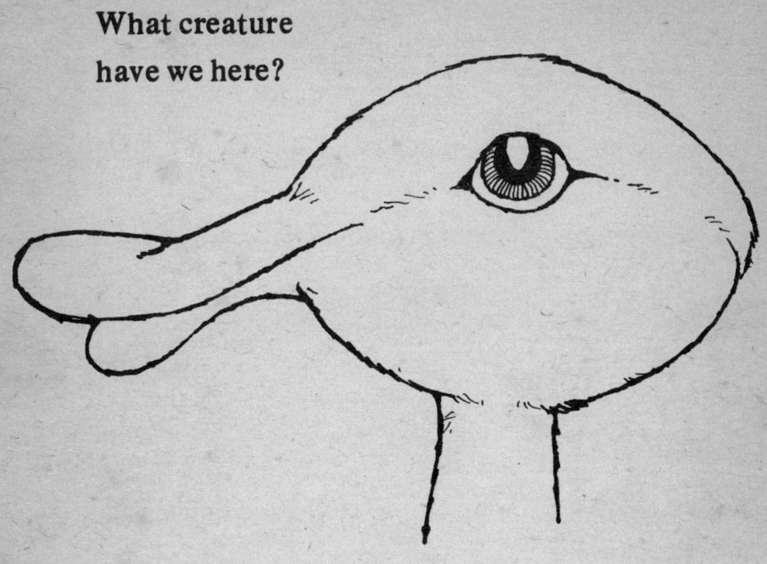

If you said a rabbit you were quite right.

If you said a duck you were quite right too!

It all depends on whether the left part of the picture strikes you as being a duck's bill before it strikes you as being a rabbit's ears.

STRANGE CIRCLES

Which of the three rings is a perfect circle?

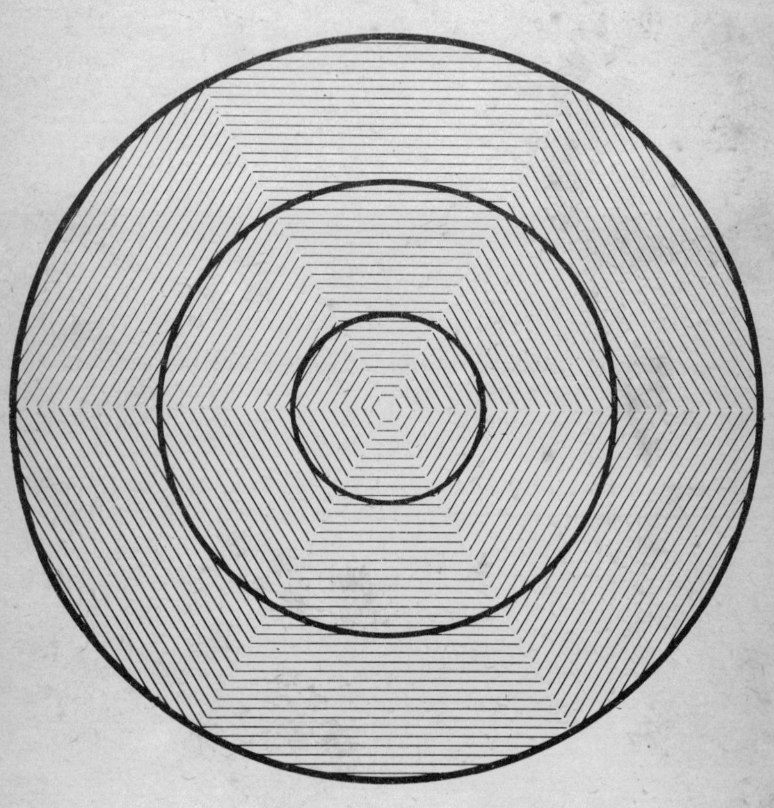

All three are! It is the background pattern that makes the perfect circles seem distorted.

TOPSY

TURVY

Look carefully at this picture by the great Dutch artist Verbeek—then turn it upside down and give yourself a surprise.

Just as he reaches a small grassy point of land, another fish attacks him, lashing furiously with his tail.

STAIRCASE

Look at these stairs any way you like and you'll still feel you could climb them. Whether you look at the page as it is or turn it sideways or turn it upside down, you'll still find stairs to climb.

It's amazing—so amazing, in fact, that it's a maze as well as an eye-teaser. Go in at one arrow and see how long it takes you to come out at the other.

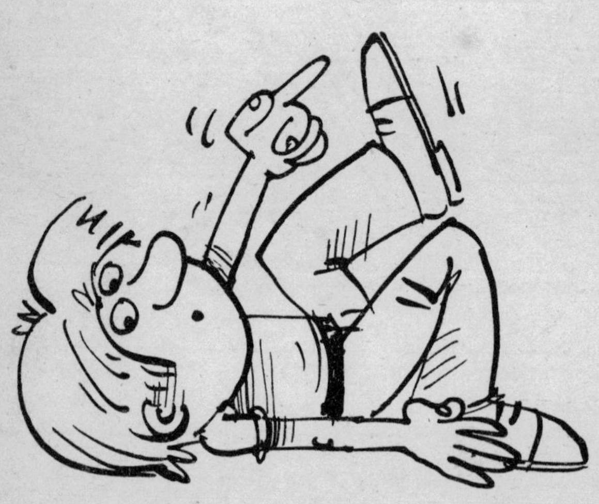

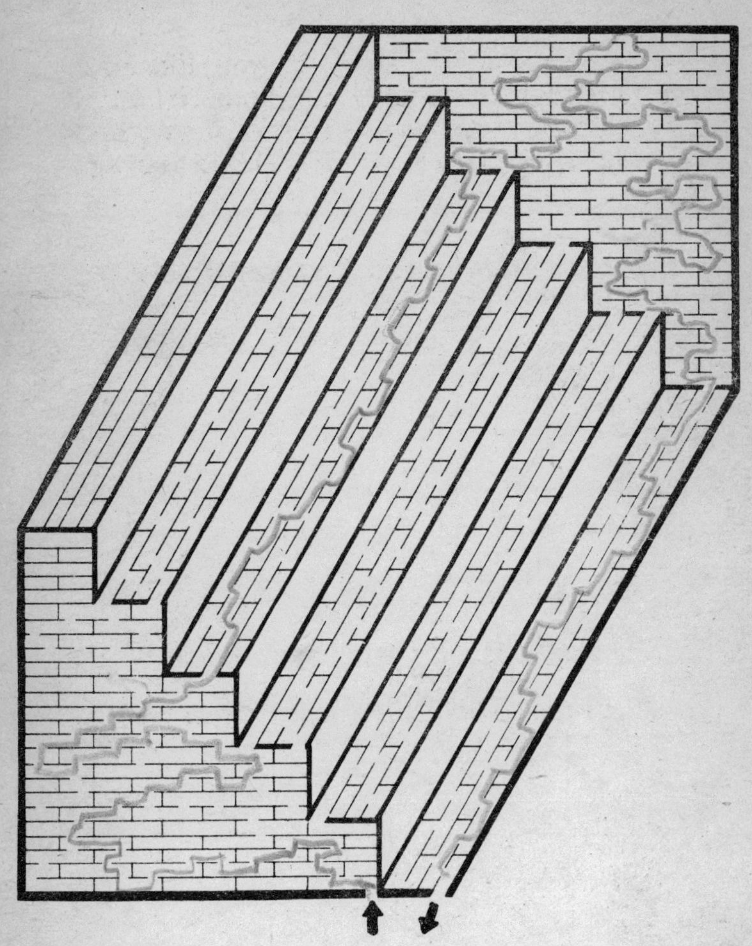

PORTRAIT OF A LADY

What can you see
in this picture?

Is it a drawing of a very old lady?

Or is it a picture of a pretty girl with her head turned slightly away from us?

It's both. Look at the picture long enough and you'll see the old lady at one moment and the girl the next.

AMAZING HAT

Here's a high hat. In centimetres how much greater is its height than its width?

The height of the hat and the width of the brim are identical — vertical lines often seem longer than horizontal lines of the same length. And it's not just an amazing optical illusion, it's an amazing maze as well. Try going in at one arrow and coming out at the other.

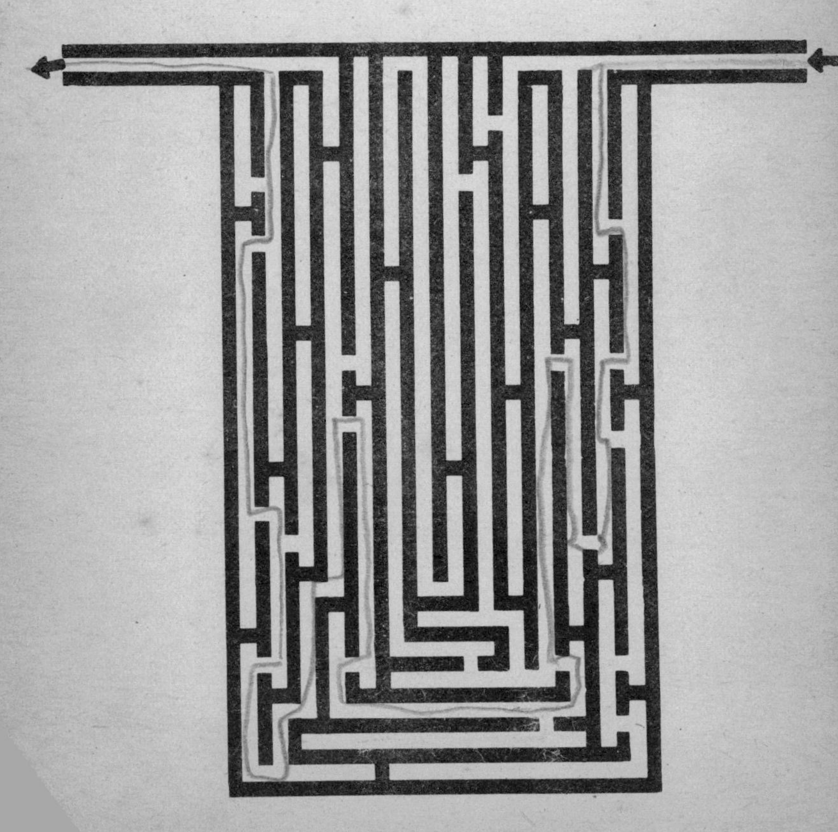